BLUE POPₗ

Blue Poppy

Ilona Martonfi

Coracle Press

Printed in a limited edition by:

Coracle Press
Box 56005
Montreal, QC
H3Z 3G3
www.coraclepress.com

Front and back cover photographs from author's family archives.
Editing and book design by Carolyn Zonailo and Stephen Morrissey.
Typeset by Richard Olafson, Victoria, B.C.
Printed and bound in Canada.

The author wishes to thank *The Montreal Poetry Group*: Janet Pasternak, Anne Cimon, Eileen Ballard, Hannah Franklin, Simon Gamsa, and Jean Carriere, for support. Thanks to Janet Pasternak for friendship and editorial help. Thank you to Carolyn Zonailo for mentoring, encouragement, and editing this collection. A special thank you to Richard Olafson for typesetting, layout, and cover design. A heartfelt appreciation to Stephen Morrissey, at Coracle Press, for his dedication in bringing this book into publication.

Library and Archives Canada Cataloguing in Publication

Martonfi, Ilona, 1942-
 Blue poppy / Ilona Martonfi.

Poems.
ISBN 978-0-9687599-3-6

 1. Abused women--Poetry. I. Title.

PS8626.A7795B58 2009   C811'.6   C2008-904275-1

This book is dedicated
to my mother
Elvira Magda Kovacs

CONTENTS

NIGHT WEDDING

RIVER STONES

ACACIA AND BONES

Night Wedding

THE APPLE TREE

The apple tree in my front yard,
I bought it from Jasmin Garden Centre.
Had it delivered by truck
with purple burlap over its roots.
I prepared a three-foot deep hole: poured in
a pail of cold water. Unwrapped the roots.

That night we made love
in front of our neighbours,
the squirrels and the tulips.
My billowing white dress hitched up
to reveal a blue garter belt.
You lifted my skirt
to rip off the sash.
With your fine teeth,
you pulled off my virginity.
Later that night
around midnight we sat,
bleeding red tulips
fell from your jacket.
Today we are man and wife.
In the windows gleam
fuchsia geraniums
with yellow dandelions.

Oleandro

Dust rises on the unpaved road to Termini Imerese. Prickly
pear cacti root in sandy areas: juicy, green to dull purple, edible
berry fruit. Fuchsia oleander, evergreen poisonous shrubs.
The whole island is an immense orchard of orange, lemon,
and olive trees. Vineyards. We take a taxi from the railway
station to the cemetery. Women in bright clothes sit by their
front doors: needlework in their hands. Small-town gossip.
The Sicilian dialect. Hills, sirocco-scorched.
The azure of the Mediterranean. A farmer with a mule
and a cart selling fresh fava beans. Fish sellers yell.
Children are called to in high-pitched voices.

Tile-roofed stone houses rise layer on layer against a ridge.
Newly painted in shades of pale yellow, brown and red ochre.
Cobalt-blue wooden balconies. My husband buys a bouquet
of brilliant gladioli at a stand: pays eight lire. His parents
are buried in the family plot. Etched in white marble are names.
Framed sepia photographs. Columnar cypresses mourn beside
a sandstone wall. His mother died at seventy-six of Parkinson's.
Two years later, his father died in his sleep, at eighty-seven. He
finds a vase and a water tap: arranges the flowers on the tomb.
We pray in silence. Our children pray.

We visit his sister and brother-in-law, in their *tabaccheria*
on the piazza. Old men in black play *scopa*. Sit idle
on fieldstone benches. Dark grey-green leaves of date palms.
"What's the matter with you?" my brother-in-law asks.
I don't answer: my husband has a mistress.
He batters me. I want a divorce.
We are invited for dinner, at their condominium: pasta with
tomato sauce. Grilled beefsteak. Fried aubergine. Salad.
Watermelon. *Granita di limone.* Up three flights of marble stairs:
pine shutters. Thick whitewashed walls cool the noon heat.
From an old stone balcony next door hang bedsheets.

Cefalu Village

Forty steps leading to a beach below the cliff. I walk on
white sand. Tell the sea my pain: my husband has his own
room. Tangiers, Barcelona, Rome, Nice, and Cefalu. Crickets
in the underbrush. Zigzagging neon on a discothèque rooftop.

I am alone on the beach. Head for the stairs. Cross the road.
See a man sitting on his parked motor scooter. "*Signora!*"
He gets off; walks rapidly towards me. "*Signora!*" The leather
soles of my black sandals echo on the cement steps:
"Clop. Clop."

I check the distance: he is bounding up the stairs. Gaining.
I reach the top. Run along the dirt road behind the hotel patio.
Scent of *oleandro,* poisonous flowering shrubs. Azure swimming
pool. Disco music. He is behind me. I run onto the terrace.

The door to the lobby is wide open: hotel clerks. Tourists. I sit
down on a bench beneath a grapevine. Red-orange geraniums.
Pot-bellied clay pots. Where our daughters find me: "Mama,
we saw you running very fast." "This man was chasing me!"

I see my husband sitting on the terrace. "Do you want to
dance?" I refuse. He dances with a strange woman. Slow dance
music is playing. I move to another table. My fingernails dig
my right arm. I go deeper, draw blood.

Paris, Summer 1989

"I'll throw you down the elevator shaft, if you divorce me!"
I stared at the iron grill. I could see inside the shaft: cables
dangled three floors down. The day before we left Paris, we
went sightseeing. Our children visited the Musée d'Orsay.

He flirted with a young Parisienne while he checked the city
map. "We'll go to the Père Lachaise cemetery," he decided.
"We'll walk there." We looked at new graves and an old open
grave with the marble slab removed: it was several feet deep.

A sunken container in the earth. The grave was empty.
"No one would be found here," he remarked. "The place is
too big." Ivy-covered stone walls. Paris traffic. August in Paris.
"Are you hungry? Let's go to that restaurant across the street."

We had spaghetti and meatballs with fresh basil. A glass of red
wine. That evening we sat across from each other on a terrace
café. The silence spilled over a blue-green chequered cloth.
Stoneware mug of black coffee. At the hotel, he surprised me:

"Sleep in my room. We have to look normal." On the last day
in Paris, we made love in the morning. Two maids knocked
with the breakfast tray. He opened the door to take the coffee
and croissants. He gave them a big grin: he was naked.

At home, he sweet-talked me: "I like your tan," he teased.
"Don't believe him," our children said. Every night after supper,
he left the house as before. I slept for five weeks on the putty-
coloured couch in the solarium. In October, I left.

A Battered Wife

I must leave you tonight.

No. I will stay. Unpack the bags and love
us once more, tonight.
Tonight I will not go.
I will not go and leave us, tonight.

Love us once more.
Tonight I will not go.

Unpack the bags. Hang up the blouses and skirts.

I will not leave with my closet half-empty:
my five fur coats, my diamonds, my 18-karat gold,
our four children sleeping in their beds
upstairs.

Ilona Martonfi   15

To My Husband

I carry your ring,
the wedding band you threw on the floor and it
rolled a little: it lay on the floor. Then I picked it
up. Then I held it.

THE PHOTO OF MRS. D.

On the red brick wall: shape of a child's hand. Green ink
on burlap: son made in kindergarten. Daughter's crewel
stitching of a meadow: ox-eye daisy and black-eyed Susan.
I smile for the photo he took in our typewriter store.

I'm wearing a russet silk skirt, short-sleeved cotton indigo
t-shirt and shell necklace: souvenirs from Italy. We took
vacations in Europe and North Africa with our four children.
Clock in mahogany: a gift for his forty-fourth birthday.

Mounted on sturdy metal wire: cherrywood carving of
myth-inspired youth and galloping horses. Five-by-six-foot
city of Montreal cardboard map. Hooked wool rug: pumpkin-
orange, dark chocolate, and white centre.

A Kiwanis Club plaque: he was honoured as the outgoing
president. What you don't see: blue Canon copiers, calculators,
cheque writers, IBM Selectrics, cash registers, filing cabinets,
desks, and chairs. A burglar alarm system.

Wrought iron grille on windows and doors. Two neon signs
on exterior grey stonewall: *Centre de la Machine à Écrire: Vente,
Location et Service. Tout pour le Bureau.* 3412 est, Ste-Catherine.
Fenced black asphalt backyard. Parked: a tan Ford van.

Down one flight of stairs, the service department. My husband
and two technicians go on the road. I work full-time in the
store. A family business moved to Hochelaga triplex. Deed
notarized, 1969. In the apartment upstairs, he beat me.

RUE ST-ANDRÉ

He wore the aftershave
I gave him last Christmas.

The turtleneck and suede jacket
I bought for his birthday.

He wore the tan trench coat
I bought for him,

the night I found him with her.

It was a bit long, the coat.

We stood there on the sidewalk,
my husband and I

in front of her apartment building.

"Shorty, I will divorce you," I said.

"I will divorce you!"

I Promessi Sposi

I carry our unborn child
into the mustard yellow car you drive.
To the smell of mothballs on your jacket.
I carry our child to your words:
"Is two hundred dollars enough for an abortion?"

I carry my child to work at Bell:
from eight o'clock until five,
I wear two girdles to hide my stomach.
The company nurse says: "Why don't you
give up your baby for adoption?"

I carry my child to the bridal shower.
My co-workers toast the bride.
Dinner and corsage at the Maritime Plaza Hotel:
crystal milk-and-sugar set wedding gift.
Don't tell them I carry a child.

I carry my child to shop at Sposabella.
Buy a silk taffeta wedding dress.
Lilies-of-the-valley bridal bouquet.
Veil and short cotton gloves.
Carry the cardboard box home.

I carry my child to the hairdresser,
the night before our nuptials.
"*Mio fratello,*" your sister says.
"My brother left town."
"*Puttana Ungherese!*" she adds. "Hungarian whore!"

I carry our child from my parents' house.
Don't tell them: "I am getting married."
I carry my child to the night wedding.
The priest doesn't say:
"You may now kiss the bride."

Night Wedding

I didn't say goodbye to my father.
I didn't see Mother in the house.
I didn't wear a wedding dress,
blossoms in my hair.

I said: "I will meet my fiancé at six o'clock."
I saw I was not loved or wooed.
I took the 55 bus on St-Lawrence Boulevard,
wearing a red fall coat and a white silk hat.
The gold wedding bands in my pocket.

I didn't kiss my betrothed at the church door.
I didn't bring a witness or a bouquet of roses.
I didn't forget he jilted me twice.

At exactly six, he drove into the parking lot.
"Were you worried?" he said, grinning.
"I had to go to the garage for a noise in the car."
"You look like a nurse in that hat."
"Let's go, and tell the priest we're getting married."

I said: "With this ring, I thee wed. I will love
and honour you for all the days of my life."

We celebrated in a five-dollar-a-night motel room.
I was already pregnant with our child.

THE CANDELABRA

In Turin park, old men in black played bocce.

We rented a furnished apartment
across from the Jean Talon Hospital,
where I gave birth to our first child.
You stayed in the labour room.
Told me: "You are beautiful."

"She was a blue baby.
The birth stopped," my doctor said.
"I used forceps on her."

In Turin park, old men in black played bocce.

You ordered me not to talk to my mother,
sister Erna, my friend Sylvia. I cooked.
I baked birthday cakes. Cut recipes from
magazines. Asked your sister:
"La ricetta per lasagna?"

Ochre brown stoneware dishes. Red wine
glasses. Your mother's wedding gift: a silver
candelabra. A parcel from Termini Imerese, tied
and knotted with plain cord.

We chose your niece, *madrina.*
A white crib with embroidered sheets.

Our daughter was one week old,
you slapped me with the baby in my arms:
"For razor stubble in the sink."

On your record player,
you played Beethoven's Ninth Symphony.

HOMECOMING

You, the soldier on the Hegyeshalom border crossing.
Winter sky, casket grey. Tall meadow grass. Fields give way
to pine forest. Dark. Fragrant. You, with the rifle! Checking my
visa, page 13. Interrogating us for over an hour. My husband is
Italian. Domicile: Montreal. I was born in Budapest, during a
February snowstorm, in the middle of World War II. *Passaporto*
photo: brown eyes, brown hair, no visible marks. Profession:
housewife. Our daughters were born in Canada: seven, five,
and three years old.

You, the nameless official, put your stamp here. I am visiting
my homeland after twenty-eight years of absence. I want to
drive through the countryside: the same road Father took on his
trek to Austria, April 1945. Squeezed into the front of his Opel
truck: mother, three daughters, and grandmother Kisanyuka.
Piled in the back, trunks and beds. Cross-stitch tablecloths,
down feather comforters. Several neighbours and friends.

A large winter landscape: snow-covered fields. Charcoal
grey leaves and brown roots. Sometimes a *falu,* a hamlet. I
could almost hear the children laughing. Playing ball in a lane. A
farmer on his horse-drawn wagon. Village women wearing drab
clothes. Travelling dirt roads on squeaky bicycles.

This was in Budapest, the second Sunday of January, 1973:
the Danube River obscured by leaden fog. Car horns blaring.
Bright yellow streetcars. We found a small restaurant. Soldiers
walked in and out of the diner. Sat nearby while we ate lunch:
goulash and *galuska.* Sweet-sour cucumber salad. Glass of wine.
Ground chestnuts with dollops of cream.

Bucharest

Sun piercing the saffron haze. Grandmothers in long black
dresses. Children laughing. Petunias in window boxes. Stopover
in a suburb of Bucharest, late July, 1975.

Across from the train, I watch a railwayman climb out through
an opening in the railcar. He stands up on the grey-brown metal
roof. Steadying himself on the domed top. His head touches a
wire. A big burly man, he flies through the air. Lands on the
cement ramp.

Singed denims slashed from top to bottom. Bloated: face,
torso and legs. Eyes closed. Wheat-coloured hair. Security
personnel walk gingerly around the body.

Glimpses of barbed wire and guards. Romania under
Communist rule. Red tape. Our railway carriage doors and
windows are locked. "You can't open them," the conductor
tells us. Half an hour later, our train pulls out of the station.

Through The Window

So, I keep going back to emptiness. I am alone, not lonely.
Then I have one simple vision: I see myself. "I will divorce you,"
he says. I am bruised and battered and in shock. Close
the bedroom door. Pull aside the white lace curtain:

eerie quiet. Grey broken fence lying on the ground. Meadow
grass covers the parched earth. Wild rose. The garden,
deserted. The silence: no birds singing. No sign of life.
Everyone left the house. Not a robin. Not even the wind.

The family that lived here, left. Nobody lives here anymore.
This is a profound feeling, a big feeling. I know I have to stay
true to that one vision. I am frightened. I don't want it. The
curtain falls from my hand. I don't want to see.

THE RED BENCH

You slapped me three days
before the birth of our fourth child.
I walked into the late November garden
and sat on the red bench covered with snow.

"The cervix is dilated," the doctor had told us.
"The birth will be any day now."

Long-sleeved blue nightgown and slippers,
wind-child howling in a black spruce.
If I sit here long enough, I thought,
I will die of the cold.

I had locked the back door
you told me not to lock.
In my sleep, I heard knocking.
Hurried up the stairs with my big belly
and child. With our sleepy-eyed child,
I opened the door.

The Dinner

He stood up quickly and walked towards me with the wine
bottle. And poured the red wine on my head. Inside this home,
our three daughters, newborn son, mother and father. On a
Sunday around noon: the air filled with woodsmoke and the
smell of chestnuts. Freshly baked bread, one of the children's
music tapes playing. Red brick house: yellow stucco, long
windows, narrow green shutters and tiled roof. Through the
printed blue cotton curtains: partial view of an evergreen tree,
snowdrift obscuring its roots. Two cords of stacked wood. The
garden's stone staircase.

The wine on my head. Crystal wine glasses. The cross-stitch
linen tablecloth. The vegetable soup. Veal scaloppini. Steamed
artichokes. Tossed salad. Black stuffed olives. Pecorino cheese.
He said: "I want my parents to emigrate from Sicily and live
with us." I hesitated too long: his mother ill with Parkinson's.
His father in his eighties. I worked full-time in our typewriter
store. Weekend cabin in St-Calixte: snowshoeing.
Tobogganing. Four children. German shepherd, Fido.

He poured the wine on my head. I sat soaked. My hair. My
eyelids. My face. He stood over me and poured. The wine ran
down: wine on my cheekbones. Food left on stoneware plates.
Wine trickling onto my lap. Olive green upholstered chair.
Soaked in wine. Until, I got up and washed my face and hair.
Scraped food from plates. Washed the dishes. Blue-painted
cupboard. Embroidered flower picture. The quilt patched
together. Winter blooms: a paper-white narcissus.
Purple mauve of the sky. The habit of silence.

Maria Kovacs

—March 25, 1897 - February 8, 1981

I just want to know where your grave is.
I want to have somewhere to put flowers and pray.

I imagined sitting beside you, Grandmother:
"My husband beats me.
Ordered me not to speak to my family."

You died of diabetes
after one year in Saint-Jérôme Hospital,
in the Laurentian mountains.

Words to your daughter, Magda:
"*Itt vagy?* Are you here?"

Magda visited you twice a week
with her husband Josef.
Sundays and Thursdays.
Brought you rice pudding, a ripe banana.
Father stayed in the corridor:
he didn't like the smell in the room.

Potted winter jasmine with yellow flowers.
Spirit masks hiding in the grove:

a choir singing *Ave Maria,*
you were cremated.
"That's all we could afford,"
Mother said.

Years later I wanted to know:
"Did Kisanyuka ask about me?"
Mama didn't answer.

THE SEVILLA BULLFIGHT

On a sunny afternoon
we cheered
with our children
we watched the bull die
dragged away
the rope
taut around its neck
in the arena
it fell
the crowd clapped
we bought leather bags
on the beach
from a peddler
we travel in its
skin
blood surging from his
mouth
the bull fell to his knees
I didn't want to watch

A Cup Of Tea With Lemon

You came back after midnight,
as you did every night
for two years you went out
after supper,
you opened the door
you walked out of the house
locked the side door
unlocked your Olds
started the motor
pulled out of the driveway
backed into the street
drove off in the direction
of downtown
to collect the rent money
to check for water damage
to rent another loft
to sign a lease
you said: "I will collect
the money on Frontenac
then go and play a game of *scopa*
with Mimmo the barber"
and I believed you
in the house on Curé-Clermont,
where I waited for you
with our four children
every night I knitted sweaters,
read self-help books
I waited and waited
for you to come back home
to open the door
to switch on the lights
walk into the bedroom
ask for: "A cup of tea
with lemon and one teaspoon of sugar."

Family Wedding

The family gathered
on the wedding day of our daughter:
in the morning we dressed,
drove in limousines to church.

Wildflowers for my daughter's bouquet,
roses and satin ribbons for her hair,
silk taffeta gown, silvery white.

She was beautiful on her father's arm:
he walked her down the aisle,
lifted the veil, kissed her,
and gave her away.

Organ music and church bells ringing,
nuns' voices sang *Ave Maria*.

"Shalom, shalom."

Maid of honour, best man.
Three ushers. Bridesmaids.
Groom's sister in vivid crimson.
Our son, the ring bearer.

Our last family portrait.

Invited, over a hundred guests,
friends and family roaring: "Kiss, kiss!"
Bride and groom stood up and responded
with deep, serious kisses.

On the wedding day of our daughter,
we danced together the tarantella.

RIVER STONES

Take The Hand Of A Child

I taught them to listen to the seagulls, before the clomp
and hiss of exhaust fumes join the sparrows. An overcast sky.
A crow. The white flowering acacia. The scent.

I taught them to go to university. Paint until the early hours
of the morning. Hang a stocking from the marble fireplace.

The house, a red brick bungalow: a home of silent rooms full
of corners. The only time my husband spoke directly to me
was to mock me. A brutal marriage, this: not a desert, but close.

Cerulean swimming pool. Raspberry bushes. Walled garden.
One day in October, I left everything standing.

I taught them to cook spaghetti with sauce: strain tomatoes.
Fry onions, light brown. Add tomato puree, pinch of sugar.
Salt and pepper to taste. Broil lamb chops. Steam artichokes.
Bake apple pies.

Purple lilac bush. Two apple trees. Red skipping rope. Three
daughters and one son.

I taught them to crochet, knit pullovers, petit point. Buy
designer clothes. Shop in the Anjou malls. Charge on credit
cards. Yell back at their father.

Cape Cod beach and seaweed. Wild roses rooted in sand.
Europe by rail together with our children: baguettes, sliced
Swiss cheese, prosciutto, and seedless grapes. Canned sardines.

THE GIFT

"Open your Christmas gift,"
I shout above
the MacDonald's din.
My grandson
unwraps a torn box:
pulls out a photo of his mother
set in a pink oval frame.
He doesn't remember her
the way his two sisters do. He was
five months old when his daddy
served divorce papers.
She had to leave three young children,
five days before Christmas.
They run and jump
in the playroom.
My daughter sees them
every two weeks
under my supervision.
She buys
French fries,
double-decker
hamburgers,
apple juice,
chocolate sundaes.
The four
of them
eat,
dunk
the fries
one by one,
into red
gooey ketchup.

THE RED FOREST *

Wildlife has reclaimed the hundreds of square miles
of abandoned land in the exclusion zone of Chernobyl.

Creeping perennial meadow grass.
Walled garden on Curé-Clermont Avenue, our former
family house: the ghostly arms of raspberry bushes.
Wild poppies. The sky there a purplish grey,
as if a storm was coming.

More than a hundred wolves prowl the forest, endangered
black storks and white-tailed eagles nest in the marshes,
and several dozen wild horses are thriving.

When in daydreams I return to Anjou,
the scene is always the same. It is a September day
when school starts: the days cool, and maples turn
a riot of yellow, scarlet, bright red. And I am sending
our four children off to school.

To normalize the abnormal.

Pines are reclaiming the Red Forest, stunted and deformed,
with unnaturally short or long needles.

Pink rhododendrons. Apple trees. In the house,
if you have any imagination, you may hear a terrible cry:
the terror, the violence that inspired my fleeing.

Forsythia are pushing up through the concrete.
Clusters of moss in the cracks.

The family that lived here, left.
Nobody lives here anymore.

* *After an article in the National Geographic, April 2006*

I, Myself, Fled Into Exile

I didn't say goodbye to my husband.
I didn't see him in the house.
I didn't wear a silk taffeta dress
or blossoms in my hair.

I said: "I am going to see a movie."
Took my black leather jacket and left.
Walked to the Honoré-Beaugrand metro.

I didn't kiss him at the side door.
I didn't bring our four children as witness
or a bouquet of long-stemmed red roses.
I didn't forget he had a lover,
slapped me twice, the month before.

As I looked back, I saw he followed me.
He said: "I could push these keys into your throat
and you'd be dead. Get back into the house."

Tile-roofed bungalow. Two apple trees.
Our children came outside and surrounded me.
The children protected me.

First Saturday of October, it was nearly ten.

Abruptly, he turned around and left.
Started the motor of his Oldsmobile
and backed out of the driveway.

I went to sit on a bench in the walled garden.
I found our twelve year old son, who told me to leave.

I didn't wash the supper dishes.
I didn't water the fuchsia geraniums.

I didn't call out: "Children, lock the door!"

WHEN MOTHER LEFT

What will I tell my teacher,
when I walk into class?

What will I do for breakfast?
What should I wear?

Father will beat you
for leaving the house.

When you leave us,
can I go with you?
Carry your bags?

I will lend you my wool mittens.

When you leave us,
call right away.
I need to know where you stay.

Mama, where will you sleep?

How can I sleep?
Go to school in the morning?

Mama, when you leave us
Father will be angry. Ask us:
"Do you know where your mother is?"

Refuge

Do you want to peel potatoes with me
in the battered women's shelter kitchen?

Do you want to see the police bring Maria
into the shelter during the night? She was a Greek woman.
Her son, George, died in jail because of "candies."

Do you want to meet the older woman with white hair?
She arrived with a large brown suitcase, brought in late at night
by the cops. Her husband beat her with wooden coat hangers.
Three days later she went back to him.

Do you want to meet with my case worker in her office?
She will ask: "How often were you battered? One time? Five
times? Ten times? Fifty times? More than a thousand times?"

I answered: "More than a thousand times."

Do you want to meet Tara, the two-year-old girl?
Her pregnant mother and I shared a room. The first Saturday
of December, it was nearly two a.m., the police picked up
the toddler. Her mom hadn't returned to the shelter by
suppertime.

The child was taken into Youth Protection custody. Do you
want to see her at night? Sleepy-eyed. Not crying.
Sleepy, in her pink pyjamas.

DIVISION OF PROPERTY

He kept the camera, photo albums, and home movies. He kept
the bronze medallion of his profile, made by a Sicilian artisan.
He kept his books. The sauna. He kept the family house in
Anjou. Our rental properties: five apartment blocks, lofts, and
commercial spaces. The chalet in St-Calixte. I took my gold
jewellery, my diamond ring. Five fur coats. Cobalt-blue
stoneware dishes. The dragonfly tiffany lamp. Twenty petit
point. The putty-coloured couch set. Grandmother's duvet.

Three days after I left, he said to our children: "Give me your
mother's number at the women's shelter. Otherwise, you have
to leave the house by six o'clock!" Two grown-up daughters,
twelve-year-old son, left their father's house. Moved in with
their pregnant married sister. A friend helped them move with
her car: loaded beds and mattresses. Comic books, easel, and
canvases. He went to the police. He accused them of theft. He
loaded the furniture into his van and brought it back home.

He kept the rental revenues. The money from a property sale.
After I left, I saw him in our Hochelaga office. He showed me
thirty-five thousand dollars cash in a handkerchief. When the
chalet burned, he kept the twenty-three thousand dollars fire
insurance. He kept the two thousand dollars for the land. I did
the company books: negotiated mortgage renewals. Opened
my own account, the first in twenty-four years. He kept the
leather couch, loveseat, and armchair. The brass king-size bed.

He kept the white Oldsmobile. The tan Ford van. He kept
the money for the grey Pontiac that he sold for one thousand
dollars. He kept the one thousand dollars for the Willis piano.
We decided, out-of-court, shared custody for our minor son.
"Give me the house keys and the alarm system keys!" he said.
I gave him the wrong keys. When he was on a two-week trip
to China, I moved a pine armoire from our former bedroom.
"It's like robbing a church!" he yelled. "But I never liked it."

Ilona Martonfi

The Moving Van

One afternoon taking the black antique hearse
to our former family house in Anjou, Jean-Pierre Rioux
turned into the driveway. The last Friday of March,
it was about two o'clock. I unlocked the side door. Switched
on the crystal chandelier.

Pale grey wood ashes in the stone fireplace. Droning
oil furnace. Up six steps to the bedroom: hardwood floors.
Empty children's rooms. Potted cacti in the solarium.
The sauna. Ice-covered swimming pool.

Six months before, I fled my home to find refuge
in a women's shelter. "Come to China with me for two weeks.
No strings attached," my ex-husband had said. "My dream is to
visit the Great Wall. Travel itinerary: Montreal, Chicago,
Tokyo, and Beijing. Stopover in Tokyo."

I chose to spend my time during his vacation to move a
pine armoire. Hiring Jean-Pierre, a Hochelaga antique dealer.
"I will take off the doors," he said. Ruddy complexion of a
woodcutter. Unkempt shoulder-length hair. Grungy jeans.

We carried the tallboy through the dining room into
the yard. Pushed it into the hearse. Threw a horse blanket
over it. He tied the "casket" down with sturdy rope.
The back door slammed shut. I took my place in the front seat.
Rolled down the window.

Up four flights of worn marble stairs: my room on Lincoln
Street. Downtown greystone. I helped lift it up the stairs.
Stopped several times to rest. Moving cost: fifty dollars, cash.

OUR TWENTY-FIFTH WEDDING ANNIVERSARY

I unwrapped the box with twenty-five long-stemmed red
roses. It was our wedding anniversary. You walked into my
bedroom and placed a long, narrow box on my antique
iron bed. You just looked at me and laughed.
Went to talk to our teenage son in his room. Then you left.

I picked up the box and took it to our former family house
on Curé-Clermont. I unlocked the side door and threw the
roses in. I heard you come downstairs, but didn't wait to talk
to you. I closed the door and left. Walked fast to the metro
station. By the time I reached my apartment, you had
brought the roses back. The box was waiting on my bed
again. This time, I beheaded them, one by one. All twenty-
five of them. And threw them into the garbage can.

I was sorry I did that.
I love red roses.

I left you a year earlier. You still brought me flowers.
"Let's go to church and renew our wedding vows," you said.
You convinced the priest to perform this holy thing: a nuptial
celebration for us, after twenty-four years of battering, four
children, and one granddaughter.

I didn't go to church with you to renew our wedding vows.
I did go out for supper with you and our children.
"Why don't you invite your mistress to join us?" I said.
"Why don't you get along for just one day?" our children said.
I drank too much wine. I was too tipsy to enjoy the dessert
of ice cream and strawberries.

ISLA DE MARGARITA

I got it on Margarita Island: looks like a rattle. Dried
pumpkin seeds inside. I bought it in the Venezuelan jungle
from a native woman: carvings of a hut, animals,
and herdsmen. Monkeys in cages.

Never a loving word. Never holding my hand.
We crossed the jungle in a Jeep, after a day on the beach.
Deep sand and coconut palms. You had said: "Let's go
to an island. See if we can get along. If not, I will give
you an amicable divorce."

In the hotel room, you swirled the rum in your mouth.
Spat twice into my face: "Now you can tell your friends,
I am not a violent man."

The third day, we took a hovercraft to Puerto La Cruz.
You gave me a gift: an ochre brown stone necklace.
We watched a black and white movie on our trip back.

The fourth, we flew to Angel Falls: the world's highest
waterfall in the Guiana Highlands. White mist and soaring
spires. I suffered a panic attack; spent the day in the hospital.

At the seafood restaurant in Porlamar, I had breaded
jumbo shrimps with a sliver of lemon. Tossed green salad.
A glass of white wine. I remember the waiter, who spoke
halting English.

You said: "Be reasonable. Come back for our son."

The sixth, you bought a necklace for your girlfriend
from the street vendor. You asked: "Which one
should I choose? The black or the white shells?"

FAMILY COURT: 4:55 P.M.

Judge: "How long ago did you leave your husband?"

Plaintiff's lawyer: "Five years."

Judge: "Have you lived with him during these five years?"

Lawyer: "No."

Judge: "How many children?"

Lawyer: "Four children."

Judge: "Patrimony?"

Lawyer: "The furniture was divided."

Judge: "Is there any chance of reconciliation?"

Lawyer: "No."

Judge: "Do you accept the divorce?"

Plaintiff: "I accept."

RIVER STONES

Our house was for sale, things buried with us.
Life in Anjou came to a shuddering end:

yellow stucco walls. Blue-painted window frames.
There in the yard, sunflowers. A solarium.
Tiled floors. Cerulean swimming pool.

The word neighbourhood still had meaning then. The
meadowland of the St. Lawrence River was wide and open:
hyacinth. The scent of wild rose. Apple tree trunks
painted white to discourage the codling moth.

In this home lived three daughters and one son, mother
and father. Sometimes I woke up at 4 a.m. just to see how
my roses looked: nude is a fabulous shade. Electric orange.
Scarlet. Desert sky.

Flowering rhododendron shrubs.
River stones. Rust red sand. Scarlet or aubergine.

But what of black's starkness?

What was it with that lack of love? It did not feel right.
Worn in the wrong places. That is, my body: smooth skin
mottled purple with bruising. A battered wife.

Comforted myself with a cup of salted tea. Knitting sweaters.
Reading self-help books. Shopping. Work. Prayer.

The last summer marked our twenty-fourth wedding
anniversary. He was a short man, middle-aged. He took up with
a pattern cutter in a factory. Seedy Montreal nightlife.

My Hochelaga Loft

The first week of November, a Saturday night,
thieves sawed off the doorknob in the glass door.
Stole my full-length mink coat
made from black male mink.
Took the television, the microwave,
my son's computer games.
The feather duvet grandmother sewed.

That first week of November,
I took the Voyageur bus with my son,
to Father's house in Tillsonburg, Ontario.
My sister Erna was visiting from Los Angeles.
I hadn't seen her for over twenty years.

The thieves sawed off the doorknob.

Left a round hole.
The front door wide open.

My ground floor loft, no running water.
Squeaky, antique iron double bed.
Our daughters' oil paintings. Terracotta brick walls.
A rental property still owned with my ex.
I called him late that night.
He brought a red metal tool box.
He came accompanied by his girlfriend.
"You could have had your throat cut!"

Mount Royal Lookout

You, the man across the river.
How long has it been
since I fled our home?

You went to see her, the night I left.

I went to sit in the garden.
I didn't water the wild roses.
Didn't pick a reed basket of apples.

You, the man across the river.
I didn't say goodbye to you.

Our children are grown-up now.
Our son had a bicycle accident last year,
on downtown Sainte-Catherine Street.
Not one person asked him: "Are you all right?"

He sat on the green couch in my studio.
Covered his face with both hands:
"I've ruined my life," he sobbed.

"Give your bike away.
Don't ride it in the city!
I want you to be an old man.
Live to be eighty."

Nine years, since he talked to you.

You, the mute man across the river.
I sit on a bench at the lookout:
water drips into the silence.

ACACIA AND BONES

Visiting The Ridge

from this view, I see it better
from this perpetual angle of scarred trees

grating to find an answer

blue-white freckles and strawberry blossoms
a horsefly swishing across my face

riddled and pinned on a leaf
wild roses and blackberry bush

in a soft, white crinoline skirt
I don't know how to write the truth

the green fly on my hand
this is where home is

THE HOUSE ON POTTERS ROAD

The garden lay bare after Father got cancer,
after his feet got blue from congestive heart disease.
He stood there for the last time,
we embraced, Father and I and he said:
"Do you need anything?" because I cried.
"Mama, give her some money."
"I don't need money."
"I need to hug you, Father, with your blue feet."

In the house on Potters Road,
"Did you love Father?" I asked Mother,
after she told me on the phone:
"Your father died."

He had asked her for a cup of tea,
and then he went to sleep.

In the house on Potters Road,
where he had lived alone with Mama.
"I was with him for fifty-three years," she said.
"I got used to him."

Weddings

My mother didn't come to my wedding. She was not invited.
My grandmother Mariska didn't go to my mother's wedding

in Arad, Romania. She didn't like my father. Grandmother had
no wedding. She never married, although she had one child.

I went to our eldest daughter's wedding. Her father was there,
too. We were still married. I went to our youngest daughter's

garden wedding. She didn't invite her father. We were divorced.
I didn't accept the invitation to our second daughter's wedding,

in Palm Beach, Florida. She invited both her mother and father.
I decided not to attend. My ex-husband used to beat me.

FAUBOURG CAFÉ

Green almond sky fluted iridescent grey-blue. It's the
temperature, cooler, darker. Natural earth tones. Basic
earth shades. The potted red geranium. Apple trees are
thicker, bushier.

Nearly nine o'clock: restaurants are opening up. Montreal,
my adopted home. Winter 1954, we lived on Pine Avenue
in a brownstone. Shopped at Steinberg's grocery store.
Woolworth's. Sainte-Catherine Street and Guy.

Landed immigrant, twelve-years-old. My menses started
three months before. The first day of sixth grade in Fräulein
Stuhl's class, I thought everybody knew. The night before
my period started. Didn't tell anyone. Not my mother. Not
grandmother. I slept all night with my first period.

"It's bad blood and all girls get it," grandmother Kisanyuka said.
Mother had a half-smile. Grandmother rummaged in her sewing
basket. Found two safety pins and a rag.

"The construction workers are back," my friend says.
"The hammering has started." Scraping of chairs.
Drizzle. Music. Air conditioning whirs.
A tree sparrow pecks crumbs from ceramic tiles.
Small brownish-grey.

Four children and two miscarriages. My body has known
periods. My body has birthed. Heavy with child. My body
has felt a child. My body and menstrual flow for forty-three
years. Five hundred and sixteen months.

My Mother, Magda Kovacs

My mother used to
wear a flowered dress in summer.
She used to laugh with father at night in bed.
Breastfeed my baby brother.
Go with us to the big circus.

When Magda was a child in Romania,
she ran to her mother for a hug,
but Mariska shooed her away.

My mother used to talk about her childhood.

She used to laugh with me:
laugh out loud in her cobalt coat.
Make a lot of noise with her wooden spoons.

My mama used to love me:
she used to give me a bath on Saturdays,
in an old tin tub, in the middle of the kitchen.
She used to comb my long black hair,
part it in the middle,
braid it with red polka dot ribbons.

My mother, Magda, was a love child.

Father had died and Mother was selling the house
on Potters Road. Worn, green linoleum in the *Stube*.
Slate-grey wool blanket warming her knees.
She said: "I met my father one time, 1940.
Ludwig Hass came from his village to Arad.

I had this great urge to meet him,
when pregnant with my first."

"We stood face to face in a small room.
I thought I'd looked into a mirror."

GRETA ZOLA

"Grandma, the sun!"
Age two, she runs,
falls down, whirlwind jogs.
Picks up three sticks,
dashes to the slides.
The ice cream vendor
rings her bell.

The man with a kite says:
"Not enough wind!"
The sun glows in the haze:
smoke from the forest fires
in Northern Quebec.
The ice cream vendor
rings her bell.

The red ball in the sky.
Greta wants the sun:
"Mine. My ball!" she yells.
The kite climbs and climbs.
We leave the playground.
The sun follows us.
The ice cream vendor
rings her bell.

My granddaughter falls asleep.

Mother's Vigil

Little sister spreads a blue shawl
over Mother's green hospital gown:

feet covered with a sheet,
respiratory tube taped to Mama's chin,

blurred behind white gardenias.
Bouquet of plastic flowers
sitting on her swollen body.
"They're Mom's favourite," she says.
"Do you want to be in the photo?
For my children. So they'll remember her."

Three daughters, a son-in-law,
granddaughter Angie, crying.

Heart rate down to 45.
Jumping around to 80.

Beeping life support.

"I'm going for a bite to eat now,"
nurse Donna Lee, tells us.
"It's one a.m. now, when I come back,
we start reducing the oxygen.
We will give her morphine. She will not panic
when the death rattle starts.
The family doesn't want to see that."

Sister with the camera.
Gardenias for props.
She didn't see blind sister, Eva,
at the family meeting yesterday,
weeping in a wheelchair.
Saying her last goodbyes to Mother.

VERHOEVE FUNERAL HOME

"Mother bought the pink sweater set herself," blind sister Eva says in the funeral chapel. "I can't recognize my mother," I tell my older sister, Erna, from Los Angeles. "Mom's hair is wavy and she is wearing makeup. I'll tell the undertaker to comb her hair out." "It was our hairdresser who did it," Hector Verhoeve says. "We didn't have a photo of your mother."

"Exiled into our sinful body…" Father Charrette prays. He is from Quebec. The priest from St. Ladislaus Hungarian parish, Courtland, died recently. They are waiting for a replacement from Budapest. Erna and I pray beside mother's coffin: at the head of the oak casket are two sepia photographs of Magda and Josef on their wedding day and Magda at seventeen. A bouquet of white roses and baby's breath decorates the coffin lid. "They were Mom's favourite," Eva says.

After the prayers, the undertaker combs Mother's hair. Hector rips her lacquered hair right off the scalp. He tears out a grey gnarl and throws it on the brown carpet. "Can I do it?" Eva's daughter, Angie, offers. She combs her grandmother's hair with gentle strokes. Leaves the chapel to wash her hands. Fingers still wet, she continues to flatten Mom's hair. "Now that's my little Oma," she smiles. Her large brown eyes, serious.

"I want to tell you about Nutella," Eva jokes. "Mother craved chocolate. She ate Nutella in her room with a knife. And she took insulin." *Ave Maria, Ave Maria,* floats from my nephew's boom box. "That's Pavarotti singing, the big fat one," I blurt out. I remember calling Eva 'Fatty' in our childhood.

"When she goes to the crematorium, the casket gets burned with mother," Eva says to her husband. "The wooden cross shouldn't be burned with her. I want to have it as a keepsake." "Either way, the coffin is going to rot in the earth, or gets burned," my brother-in-law says, in his Italian accent.

MAGDA'S BLIND DAUGHTER

A photo of my mother, Magda, and sister, Eva, posing
in the house they live in. Up five stone steps. Tiled
roof and azure painted balconies. Magda's room is closed.

A bride's box with tulips. An old
wedding veil. Her blind daughter's silk taffeta dress.
The colour white. I stand at the gate of the house in London,
Ontario. The year is 2005. There in the snow-covered yard,
a catalpa tree. Bramble and nettle. Thorny blackberry bushes.

Sepia-hued photographs on a shelf:
Magda in Arad, Romania. Black leather school shoes.
Dark blue pleated skirt. White long-sleeved blouse. White
leggings.

On a Saturday in mid-February,
white roses and baby's breath. Funeral candle burning
on the kitchen counter. A scrapbook of pressed wildflowers.
I look back and see omens: dreams. A broken glass plate.

Darkness, save for blazing wood fire.
Mother died three days ago.

Up five stone steps: Eva's house with its tiled roof
and blue balconies. A collage of family photos: Magda and
Josef on their wedding day and Magda at seventeen. On the oak
table: watermelon and clementine. A potato baked with sea salt.
Four sisters weep. Brother Joe mourns on the West Coast.

Tillsonburg Cemetery winter burial: a light snow falling.
Scent of cedar and cypress trees. The Lord's Prayer. Eva,
Magda's blind daughter, ill with bronchitis, couldn't attend her
mother's funeral.

A Funeral Song For Magda

—*July 3, 1922 - February 16, 2005*

On a bitter February day
a light snow falling,
Mother is the blue sky.
Bare catalpa tree:
seed pods rattle in the wind
in my blind sister's backyard.

Mother is the water
washing her daughters' hair.
Laughing and crying,
in my blind sister's kitchen.

Mother is the body I carry,
twelve white roses and baby's breath.

Silver-grey hearse.
Cars and lorries pull over:
a small-town tradition.
Cornstalks and funeral flags.

Mother is the railway crossing:
a cemetery on the right.
Six pallbearers and requiem choir.
Purple glass bead rosary.
A *Hail Mary* full of grace,
in my blind sister's voice.

Mother is the empty room
we didn't enter for ten days,
in my blind sister's house.

My Mother Used To

comb my hair, braid my hair
she touched my hair: so did the teacher

she used to pull my white knee socks
up and up over my knees: right up to my neck
I sat in a knee sock
she was hidden, my mother, in my sock
she spoke little to me

GIPSHAND

"She lost her right hand in a threshing
machine. A farm accident," they say.
A round, white gypsum hand sticks
out of a coat sleeve. "Open the gate
for me, please," she says. I lift the
iron latch.

War refugees from Budapest:
father and mother, three young
daughters, grandmother Kisanyuka.

A farmer in Schillerswiesen
gives us one room at the back of his
house: a common room equipped with
a wood stove for cooking, a table, and a
few single beds.

Deep in the Bavarian Forest: a large
blue dragonfly. Dandelions. Wild violets.
Raspberry bushes. Blueberries.

Rooted in a treeless clearing:
white wooden cross for a soldier.

THE SHAPE OF THE STREET

Splinters of snow-glass
lay on the grass
red poppies grew in bomb craters

in the noise
in the house

father killed our dog, Beno,
with a sledgehammer
he put a potato bag over him
and jammed him into a vise
Beno had bitten two people
our grandmother, also

—*Neutraubling, Germany 1951*

FOURTH GRADE TEACHER

I had my own cot
in the morning,
mother combed my hair
she braided my black hair
I washed my face
took my school bag
walked out of the house
past the linden tree
yellow dandelions
the neighbour's strawberries
past the grocery store
I walked up the six steps
opened the door to the school
entered the classroom
went to my desk on the right—
teacher was there every morning—
I shook his hand:
"Guten Morgen Herr Lehrer!"
I can still see him
he called me up front:
"Schwarze, write on the blackboard!"
later a black and white movie flickered
on the wall,
my teacher fondled me
he stood behind me
without saying a word
I sat between two boys
in the last row on a desktop
his huge body in the dark
touched my blue flowered cotton dress,
my pigtails

EASTER SUNDAY, 1952

Red and yellow Easter eggs
chocolate rabbits in cellophane

not a sound
it was so quiet

mother lying on the rooftop
in her short-sleeved summer dress

so quiet upstairs
no sunlight

the linden tree in the yard
grandmother's wash line

pussy willows in bomb craters
an Easter lily bloomed

after my mother attempted suicide
we visited her in the hospital

I didn't know what to say to Mama
I went over to her and kissed her cheek

Weihnachten

"*O Tannenbaum, O Tannenbaum,*" Father sings in a loud voice.
Tears roll down his face: "I am crying for my mother,"
he says. Oma Rosalia, Opa Alexandru, eleven siblings,
live behind the Iron Curtain, Hungary and Romania.

It is winter in my childhood. When it snows, snow falls on the
cement stairs in the roofless hallway. The old airport
Neutraubling: *Halle 7.* A war refugee town in the foothills
of the Bavarian Forest: school. Church. Bayer's grocery.

"Make a list for St. Nicholas," Mother says. I write: fairy tale
book and dark blue ski pants. *Der Weihnachtsbaum* sparkles with
bright red candles. Angel hair, icicles, gold and green glass
ornaments. Sugar houses. Toboggans.

Hidden in the branches: *Lebkuchen,* gingerbread, walnuts,
tangerines, and apples. Hazelnut milk chocolate. Five children
sing "*Stille Nacht, heilige Nacht.*" My sister Erna gets the
ski-pants. *Christkind* brings me a book, *Hansel und Gretel.*

Grandmother sobs broken-hearted on her bed. A common
room furnished with a wood stove for cooking, a table,
a few chairs, and two single beds. A pine chest stacked with the
family's hand-embroidered tablecloths and pillowcases.

My short, plump grandmother Kisanyuka: silver braid fastened
with four metal pins into a bun. Floral housedress. Sturdy shoes.
"I miss my mother." She wipes her tears with a handkerchief:
"My mother's birthday is 24 December."

BREMERHAVEN

Why did mother slap me, when father took a young
Hungarian woman to a coffee shop in Bremerhaven?
Why did she yell at him: "I will not go with you to
Canada anymore!" Our ship was sailing the next day for
Quebec. Mother packed everything we owned into two
wood crates and shipped them by train to Bremerhaven.

We said our goodbyes. Grandmother came with us to the
train station. She hugged and kissed everyone, then she
left the railway carriage. I watched her through the grimy
window: my short, plump Kisanyuka, her silver braid
under a flowered cotton kerchief. Tears streamed down
her face. "She will join us in Montreal," father promised.

The first Monday of October, 1954, Mother told me:
"Go to school and say goodbye to your teacher."
"*Wir emigrieren nach Kanada,*" I said with a shy smile.
"We are emigrating to Canada." Sixth grade classmates
stood around Fräulein Lizelotte Stuhl's pinewood desk.
"Do you speak English?" "I don't speak English."

I said my goodbyes to my friend Ingrid. I went to see her
on her father's farm in Birkenfeld. We talked in the barn.
Bales of straw were piled high in the loft. "I will write.
Auf Wiedersehen!" That morning in Bremerhaven Mother
said: "Stay with your father and don't let him out of your
sight." Father was sitting at a cherrywood table.

He was talking fast and loud to the woman. Drinking
his coffee with schnapps. Not knowing what to do, I
watched father closely. I was eavesdropping with my
sister Eva. The oak door swung open and mother walked
into the café. She gave me a slap in the face: "You didn't
watch your father, as I told you. See what he is doing!"

ERNA'S WEDDING

Rose-pink carnations for my sister's bouquet,
pearl diadem for her hair.
Hooped crinoline silk lace gown.

She was beautiful on Father's arm:
he walked Erna down the aisle,
lifted the veil, kissed her,
and gave her hand to William.

Nuptials held at Sankt Bonifatius church,
organ music and wedding bells ringing,
the groom was Protestant, the bride, Catholic.

She'd met William at a German picnic.
In Lachute, she first saw him:
tall, curly blond hair, blue eyes,
hopping on one leg in a potato bag.

In the tent, he asked her for a dance.
Came courting in Blainville:
three months later, they married.

Our last family portrait.

Invited, over thirty guests,
at the groom's parents' house in Brossard.
Friends and family shouting: "Kiss, kiss!"

On the wedding day of my eldest sister,
I learned to dance the polka.

KISANYUKA'S DRESS

Grandmother needs a grave.
She needs a funeral.

The metal urn with her ashes sits
on a pinewood shelf in sister Eva's garage.
A fenced red-brick house. Walled garden.
Flowering acacia tree and rhododendron.

Grandmother didn't ask for anything.

After high school, I worked for Bell.
Sewed a dress by hand: "Try the dress, Kisanyuka."
Four yards of indigo print, not cut from a pattern.

"The sleeves are too long," she said.
"The skirt is too long. I'll wear it in the house."
Rolled up her sleeves: plump and five feet tall.
Worn flat shoes. Big round bunions. Ample breasts.

Grandmother planted sweet peas and radishes.
"You're so pretty!" she talked to tulips.
Named her chickens: "Pettika, Rosika, and Susie."
Collected eggs in the grey sagging barn.

Sliced up a loaf of black bread.
Kissed the bottom of the loaf:
"If we didn't have bread we couldn't live.
Many people are hungry. Bread is holy."

MARISKA'S DAUGHTER

Tightly drawn curtains in the windows of the house
made with brown ochre stone. Potted red geraniums.
The dirt roads are empty, strangely quiet. Magda's
room is closed.

Her mother's hand-embroidered muslin dress.
Eyelet petticoat, the colour purple. Sepia-hued
photographs on a shelf. Cross-stitch tablecloth
Mariska sewed.

A love child.

I stand at the gate of Mother's childhood house in
Arad, Romania. The year is 1928. A photo of Magda
posing in a studio: dressed in black leather school
shoes. Pleated dark blue skirt. White long-sleeved
blouse. White leggings.

Bees in the kitchen garden. Peach trees and pear
trees. Fleshy red berries of shrubs. Thistle and
nettle. Thorny acacia with yellow flowers. Laundry
fluttering from a wash line. Mariska works as a cook.

After school, Magda is alone in the house.
Stepfather says: "I'll kill you, if you tell anyone!"

Puppetry is her favourite childhood pastime:
everything secret.
On a Sunday in early September,
there in the cold grey yard

entwined with wildflowers.
Meadow grass. River stones.

Mama's Breast Cancer

I have a rucksack full of miracles:
shears and wool and wadding,
clips and a surgeon's scalpel.
I have an operating table, Mama.
I will perform the surgery:
dress you in a blue gown,
stretch it flat. Make it
lazy and calm. Nursery lights,
as for babies, and blues
and pinks and baby bodies.
I will not hurt. I will hold you
and give you my breast.
You will suckle and smile, and go
to sleep.

THE WALTZ

Can I have this dance with you, Mama?

Mama, let me take your hand.
Let's dance with your phantom breast.

Mama, let's dance the waltz
in your flowered summer dress.

Big band, five-piece orchestra:
flowing and melodious music.

Three-quarter time, step-step-close.
Waltz you around the floor.

We are dancing.
I love you, Mama.

Mama, thank you.

Acknowledgements

Some of the poems in this collection have appeared in the following periodicals, anthologies, online sites, and university newspapers: *Carve, Carte Blanche, Soliloquies, Arcade, Vallum, Fire With Water, Fruits of the Branch, Sun Through the Blinds: Haiku Today, Montreal Serai, Helios, The Link, The Yellow Door News*.

"The House On Potters Road" and "Visiting The Ridge," were translated into French by Élizabeth Robert and appeared in issue # 63 of the periodical *Arcade*, Montreal, Quebec, summer 2005.

Martonfi was a finalist in the 2007 Quebec Writing Competition. Her story "My Daughter, Marisa" was published in the third edition of the CBC story anthology, *In Other Words: New English Writing From Quebec* (Vehicule Press, 2008).

Some of the poems in this collection first appeared in the online and print-form chapbook, *Visiting the Ridge* (Coracle Press, 2004).

About the Author

Ilona Martonfi earned a Bachelor of Arts in Applied Human Sciences from Concordia University. She leads workshops on crisis management and personal development. Martonfi also offers creative writing workshops in poetry, prose, and memoir writing.

For the past decade, Ilona Martonfi has produced and hosted the enormously popular reading series: The Yellow Door Poetry and Prose Reading Series. Martonfi is the co-founder and host of the annual *Lovers & Others* reading. She now also presents the Visual Arts Centre's poetry and prose reading series.

Martonfi—as well as producing the above reading series—actively participates in giving readings from her own work in many venues in Montreal. She is currently working on a memoir and a second collection of poetry.